Praise for the works of Jennifer Reeser

The Lalaurie Horror

"...an amazing *terza rima* narrative of a tour through an old haunted house,
done in unnerving *Grand Guignol* style."

—*Trinacria*

Sonnets from the Dark Lady and Other Poems

"Jennifer Reeser has never lacked poetic courage...she loves literature, Louisiana, and drama. Like the languid and intense tastes of New Orleans itself, Reeser's style will take you by surprise...Her antecedents are Millay and Shakespeare, Tennessee Williams and Charles Baudelaire."

—*Mezzo Cammin*

"Compelling and metrically confident...Reeser offers surprising language and an often playful tone in this accessible, engaging collection. ..ably demonstrates why she is one of the most admired of today's younger poets writing in rhyme and meter."

—*Rattle Magazine Online*

Other books by Jennifer Reeser

The Lalaurie Horror

Sonnets from the Dark Lady and Other Poems
Finalist for the Donald Justice Prize, 2010
Winterproof

An Alabaster Flask
winner of the Word Press First Book Prize, 2003

Fleur-de-lis

by Jennifer Reeser

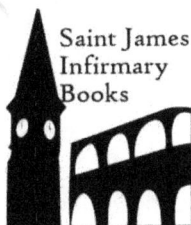

Saint James
Infirmary
Books

Cover art by Jennifer Reeser
Copyright©2016 by Jennifer Reeser

First Edition, September, 2016
Fleur-de-lis

ISBN: 978-0692766491

Saint James Infirmary Books
Sulphur, Louisiana

"Quand on veut tuer son chien on l'accuse de la rage."
"When one wants to kill the dog, one accuses it of rage."
(Old French Proverb)

FOR CHARLIE HEBDO

———

The author wishes to thank the editors
of the journals in which
these poems first appeared:

*Able Muse, Danse Macabre, First Things,
Levure Littéraire. Life and Legends,
Lucid Rhythms, Measure, Mezzo Cammin,
The National Review, Recours au Poème,
Shoes or No Shoes?, THINK Journal,
Trinacria, & The Writer*

Contents

III.From *Les Fleurs du Mal*

IV.   Paris to Orleans

Foreword

Kathryn Oliver Mills

The spirit of Baudelaire infuses Jennifer Reeser's new collection of poems, both in ten translations remarkably faithful to the originals' forms, sense, sounds, and in Reeser's own thoughtful observations of how, in both Paris and New Orleans, "the depth of life reveals itself in all its profundity in whatever one is looking at, however ordinary that spectacle might be" (Baudelaire). Like those of the 19th century *flâneur*, Reeser's 21st century city scenes can be somber and alienated. "Leathered packs with cigarettes/on precipices blowing smoke" people Sacré Coeur, where the "green, absent glare" of smashed bottles reminds that "although surrounded, one is yet alone".

However, and as the two poets' titles suggest, *Fleur de Lis* invokes *Les Fleurs du mal* to represent its own views and voice. Baudelaire's perspective moves from gritty particulars into the ether of despair or the imagination; Reeser's vantage point is often elevated—at Sacré Coeur, on a balcony, in Notre-Dame, in the contemplation of art as well as of universal problems—and from there she regularly moves towards the world, embracing its fallenness with empathy. Baudelaire's look into a passing woman's eyes opens into chasms of desperate longing; Reeser warns a woman in the metro to protect her gaze from a city's hunger. Crime roams Baudelaire's streets; Reeser describes streets "awash with soap suds."

Indeed, for Reeser there is hope for human blood's stains, in the humble work of the "Laundresse in the 6ème Arrondissement," or in the glorious windows of Notre-Dame, where each stain is "a simple stain within pure glass;/and failure, a mere panel in the panes." Reeser's lyric word-play can also illuminate dark subjects in flashes of humor that are glancing, poignant, and playful rather than mordant. At the Pantheon she quasi-comically, quasi-tragically mixes the plangent with the matter-of-fact when she declaims: "Saint Genevieve is dying on the wall./Across the marble floor, schoolchildren call"; she relates her two city loves by imagining plane trees with Spanish moss.

The range of form, emotion, and tone in this florilège is broad, and the strong narrative arc between Paris and New Orleans alchemizes the many "correspondences" of *Fleurs de Lis* into a transcontinental, trans-temporal vision. Reeser's poetic voice knows despairing rhapsody, and her world-view is shaded by Baudelairean spleen. The flowers Reeser offers us here, though, are not ultimately of suffering and evil ("mal"). They are indeed "lis," lilies symbolic of France, of New Orleans, and of life and death restored, through blood, to delicate forms of humanly flawed, fragile purity.

Summer, 2016

The Balustrade

I am an iron balustrade
erected over courtyard gates,
on which a writer ruminates,
with *fleurs de lis* and leaf motifs inlaid.

When sorrow overcomes her heart,
I hold her, like a baby's crib,
this borrower of Adam's rib,
until she comes to contemplate my art.

My metal raises her above
the revellers in bright attire,
before a tall cathedral spire,
and lovers blindly stumbling in their love.

Aslant, I settle on each pole,
complex and wrought with tortured charm --
severe, but in the sunlight, warm,
I smooth the malformations of her soul.

I. Poems of Paris

From the Balcony

I see a French flag -- thin and faded -- flying.
The European siren rarely stops.
Again, again it sounds, approaching, dying
through St. Sulpice's closed-for-Sunday shops.

Ridged solar panels have replaced some shingles,
their tinted windows add a somber charm
with sloping. Chill mid-April weather tingles
the flesh, blains raised with each police alarm.

I should pay scant attention to these skies,
those skies so similar in Moscow, Rome,
and over the Atlantic, which comprise
the whole of what makes Heaven, in my home.

This morning wind -- in character the same
as that I fled, and as yet, do not miss --
has not provoked my fear, nor borne my blame,
so bearing up my sympathy, by this.

The breath of Paris pushes at my shutters.
From where these sea gulls cry, I cannot say.
The tattered flag, in constant flux, still flutters.
The sirens ferry everything away.

French Scarves

Parisienne women don't wear hats.
They wear cloth serpents round their throats,
with leather ballerina flats.
Parisienne women don't wear hats,
but leggings snug as studded spats
beneath their cropped, hue-neutral coats.
Parisienne women don't wear hats.
They wear cloth serpents round their throats.

Versailles Ballade

The morning beams steal down the field of Mars.
The streets, awash in soap suds, smell of sage.
The people march to work, a few in cars,
and some on cycles pedal to their wage.
I pull the coverlet, roll my ribcage
towards one corner of the mattress, lie
composed as any corpse, and disengage.
I have made love in Paris. Let me die.

Aurora, Mars beside, pours out her jars,
with gravity his gun, and time his swage,
illuminating brasseries and bars,
the rooftops of Grand Garnier's opera stage.
Fed on *tartelettes* of the Chartreuse gage,
I have seen queens' swans, moved a man to cry,
heard Bach played in the Metro on guitars.
I have made love in Paris. Let me die.

Though this same sunlight reaches me, and wars
against my body, forcing it to age,
outlining its deficiencies, its scars
become italic, as upon a page,
I shall not let its insolence enrage,
but blankly only wonder with a sigh.
There is no longing left here to assuage.
I have made love in Paris. Let me die.

Revered and royal phantoms -- shahs, kings, czars
forever overshadowing Versailles
through mirrored hallways: hear me from the stars!
I have made love in Paris. Let me die.

"Pas de Sortie"

With his wicked innocence, every morning
comes the boy again to me, small and calling,
dressed in stone-washed fabric and giving warning,
"Pas de sortie là!"

Pointing back behind him, he makes advance,
off *L'Allée Royale*, with the most intense
gaze I have encountered within all France
girding his guidance.

"No way out!" It echoes -- effective lightning
through the fabled labyrinth's growing augurs –
sweet, perhaps well-meant, but yet somehow frightening,
falsely beguiling.

For the boy was smiling with foreign magic.
Maybe he believed it himself, not knowing
how the ground we walked upon there was tragic,
cursed though enchanting.

Then again, perhaps he disguised derision,
my unused umbrella a subtle signal:
here was someone destined for certain prison,
Reverie's captive.

Do I dare to speculate? Halls of mirrors
made that "dauphin" seem a reflected figure,
reminiscent of revolution's terrors:
"Pas de sortie là!"

After all, the exit indeed existed.
Far beyond, unseen from that childish vantage,
past the clean-clipped hedgerows, so nobly twisted,
opened our way out.

Still I hear his steps on the castle gravel,
see his fair, fair hair, and his French blue trousers,
feel the wind pulled after his outré travel --
rapid and crab-like.

Last Night

If one sits on the steps of Sacré Coeur
    to see the city after dusk,
one sees, too, in the cold, each traveler:
    the silk-scarved men, distinct with musk;

the ladies in flared mini-skirts and tights,
    most often black or midnight blue,
occasionally punctuated – brights,
    or puce, or some unlikely hue.

One sees the leathered packs with cigarettes
    on precipices blowing smoke.
One listens to musicians finger frets
    for famous songs, of rock or folk,

And smells some bitter *andouille* on the wind,
    grim and scraggly grass in cracks,
the perspiration of the olive-skinned,
    or warmly melted votive wax.

Green *macaron* in hand, its mellow paste
    the flavor of pistachio --
like olive skin one cannot touch nor taste --
    in vain, one fights with vertigo.

The tourists photographing from a tier
    below, curved girlfriends striking poses,
roaming vendors proffer bottled beer
    and blood-red, long-stemmed roses.

As twilight deepens, one will then observe
    deposit, these distracted brash,
the emerald, drained merchandise they serve
    in bags hung on the fence for trash.

Perhaps unnoticed, wholly by surprise,
    a bottle will miss the bag, and break,
its broken shards outspread like distant eyes
    which cause some hazel heart to ache.

Upturned and staring from the chilly stone,
    the pieces render one aware
although surrounded, one is yet alone,
    by means of their green, absent glare.

Attempting to escape from such a glower,
    one stands, walks to the west, the sight,
the tall seduction of the Eiffel Tower,
    alluring and aligned with light.

And from those heights, perhaps one then will wonder
    in silence, what it would be like
to fall beyond the fence, and tumble under
    this platform -- plentiful -- to strike

some unidentified allée, to splatter
    the ground of Sacré Coeur beneath,
and if the dizzzy mind would even matter
    to brittle bones, or grinding teeth.

Marie Antoinette's Magnolia Tree

(in *le hameau de la Reine*
château de Versailles, 2012)

Walking through the hamlet of the queen,
past cherry blossoms, lilacs, weeping willows,
wood benches set at angles, silver-green,
white daisies, blue flax, dandelion yellows,
I stopped, stunned by a lone magnolia tree --
its glossy leaves diseased and turning brown.

You would not have approved of it, Marie,
these singular disgraces in the crown.
Your garden of red rhubarb in a blur
of elevated vigor left behind,
you might have sought your squatting gardener,
and issued him a measure of your mind:
valet de pied of rebels, to allow
a foreigner this way, so southern-brow.

To the City of Light

Better outside the Orsay, in the chill and the drizzle,
walking the quai and the alleys adjacent the Louvre,
searching -- umbrella in hand -- for some delicatessen
friendly to foreign incompetence, nothing to prove.

Terrible, terrible chips shipped from shops in Great Britain
tucked in my bag, I discover a bright *boulanger*,
order a praline rose escargot pastry, brioches,
pavé suisse, paper-wrapped bread and a brownie. I pay.

Next, I return to the silent, unheated apartment,
Rue du Vieux Colombier, Old Cote Street of the Dove,
climbing five flights of a tight, spiral staircase to coffee
poured in a pink piglet mug, and those poets I love.

City of Light and Perfection, your virtues are models
filled with détente and with drama, with glamour and poise
vying for mortal affections -- my ultimate havens,
those are possessed of a conscience, with pulse, and a voice.

Pantheon

Sainte Genevieve is dying on the wall.
Across the marble floor, schoolchildren call.
Below, Rousseau will never hear at all.

This monument to Man is filled with mirth,
no mention here of sorrow nor rebirth.
This mortuary earns its money's worth.

Gargantuan glass tiles allow a glare
on fresco, column, sculpture -- everywhere --
as we descend a narrow, spiral stair.

A guard instructs the patrons to keep right.
This wealthy morgue, an imagist's delight,
has caused my chest to thicken and grow tight.

What happens when the sun of nothing sets,
Girards have gone, with Jean-Pauls and Babettes?
I feel this is as cold as coldness gets.

What unholy entities possess
these forms, in their weird blend of skin and dress,
one panel figure prim, the next, a mess?

Morts, morts, morts, morts, in gold on each wall written;
yet in this chill, not one glove, not one mitten,
not two hands wrung, nor any blue nail bitten.

Notre Dame by Night

There is no peace in Paris like this peace,
perhaps no peace like this peace in the world.
Benevolent and merciful in cast,
its corner circles twirl like tambourines
upon the stone façade, below *chimères* –
illusions of triumphant, upraised evil.
There is a peace – profound yet not transcendent –
in palaces of music, dance or art.
It is all one can ask, as far as soul,
but this is an invasion of the spirit,
completed and defeating and eternal,
wherein the fluid worship of a traveler
will neither mitigate itself, nor cease.

One feels as though this peace might travel well.
The bottle of the body being fragile
and porous, I am wondering how far –
this structure an inanimate embracing
of nature, sentimental art and pardon.
By twilight – most enamored of my sight,
how much has been remanded in such thoughts
and words as mine on this, your church, Marie?
This character and color serve as plaintiffs
of symmetry for symbolism's sake,
and each direction recognized of Time.
The future, present, past depict themselves
en rouge et noir. Each traveler this moment
appears as if to be a fresh-faced child.

The light is kind and more-so, by these candles.
Even the sore, protruding eye gains pardon
with beauty, though the penitent and sobbing
seem rare, for this prime hour, this evening's prayer.

An adolescent wanders from his group
of boys in uniform, and says to me,
"Bonjour," no angst that he might go astray,
becoming lost in this millennial city.

To lose oneself in Paris is to panic
with pleasure and a sense of optimism
unparalleled in any other place,
its blissful outskirts turning bleak, its absent
provincial postcard warmth becoming cold,
inducing an illusion of starvation.
One takes the train, returns again, the Seine
suddenly comes in liquid view, and you
might find yourself content to sink and drown.
but here, one is a traveler not lost –
heavier with hope than anywhere.

To live in Paris is – at times – to lose
encouragement to all but mere survival,
so well surrounded by the pinnacles
of humanly attainable achievement.
But returning to the Notre Dame Cathedral,
to live in Paris is – all times – to gain
a steady stimulus to the extreme,
an inspiration spiting satisfaction,
each stain a simple stain within pure glass;
and failure, a mere panel in the panes.

If one should fail in climbing to the bells,
if one should fear the topmost of the towers,
those tears shed on its tables should suffice.

A Laundresse in the 6th Arrondissement

No less fair by tinted indoor light,
she uses a distorted *saucier* spoon
to powder out the messes of the moon,
and bleaches blood stains till the sheets turn white.

The stains which – with disquiet – overnight
appeared in their misshapen splendor, soon
fade from alarming scarlet to maroon,
then innocent pink sand, to wash from sight.

Not brilliant, yet not difficult to teach,
and recognizing genius in a basic,
relinquished to this lesson from the bleach,
she finishes her business with a classic –
as influential clarifying satin
as whom she services, translating Latin.

Doves at Hôtel des Invalides
the tomb of Napoleon, Paris

Pert on the path, undisturbed by the feet of the masses,
one of them spurns its winged company, skirting an urn.
German is heard here, above the *mélange* of blurred language,
hurtling down to the turf of the vast *Champ de Mars.*
Pooled and alert, colored cream but pearl-banded with pewter
circling its neck, lurching, searching for customers' crumbs,
one of them works from the vertical frame of my camera,
deftly averting the march of Napoleon's comers.

Two of them -- rubbing like lovers -- immersed in fount water,
furtive and fat, bathe by turns on the spurted cement,
swerving, their quartz-like rose claws padding. But these two are silent,
nodding absurdly towards the removed Eiffel Tower,
nodding as though they observed its brown-burnished facade.
Miniscule, in that terse vestibule, everyone girded
under the shirred Tower arches, guarded by the *gendarmerie.*
Mammoth, outlandish – and yet, universal, one learns.

Ravens at *Cimetière de Montmartre*

One must look deeply. They appear
in flight transparent as a tear,
land on a sepulcher and pause,
resume portentous, coarse French caws,
contrary to the cooing dove.

Or else -- *au pair* -- they cling above
to nameless branches, from a twig
fragile and slick, while workmen dig,
as if another grave, white clay
along the perilous *allée.*

So unrelated to the crow
at present, unashamed to show
their fingers, fanned with glossy glee,
they pose for us – the *bourgeoisie.*

Twice I have lost my step, to twist
an ankle in this morbid mist.
And though I search and search, to save
my life, I cannot find the grave
I seek, but mounting stair to hill,
I hear the ravens call, until
they have convinced me: *Give up hope.*

The scene below me grand in scope,
deranged, at least they do not mock.

I close my rain-repellent smock,
the Gothic slabs which please me most
refusing to produce my ghost.

And so, and so…what else remains
but to enjoy these grays, these rains?
If grim, they make a stately view,
with verdigris and muted blue
uniquely labeled for this land.

Like books or black birds, I feel banned.

Degas and Berlioz, Gautier...

"Withdraw!" the ravens seem to say,
and yet, as friendly as you please,
distressed to see me on my knees,
begin again their search for food –
ruffled like me, and moist in mood.

In the Catacombs of Paris

These catacombs I roam for goodness' sake,
For sixty feet descending, rung by rung --
Six million souls in measure, and opaque.

Had I remained above, my heart would break,
For this has been a dream since I was young –
These catacombs I roam for goodness' sake.

It seems I have come home -- do I mistake?
I murmur in a forked and foreign tongue,
Six million souls in measure, and opaque.

I curl my frozen toes. My fingers ache.
A chronic malediction floods my lung.
These catacombs I roam for goodness' sake.

I stumble in the limestone lanes, but snake
As gracefully as possible among
Six million souls in measure, and – opaque,

My bones, like these, a layered wedding cake,
Romantically, grotesquely, subtly hung –
These catacombs I roam for goodness' sake,
Six million souls in measure, and opaque.

On Baudelaire's Grave

They say that Wednesday's child is full of woe,
And I was born on Wednesday; where I go,

With whom I go, what I say, what I do
Begin and end with "o" and "w."

My morning visit with him has been wet --
A wraithlike woman, blowing rose and jet.

A bottle of the Seine's scent in her bag
Has broken open, and her shoulders sag.

She nips me as I bite the metal nib
Of my blue fountain pen, his bed a crib.

"...*son beau fils,*" the father's headstone reads.
I have no Metro ticket, no bright beads

From his beloved Creole belles to give.
I kneel upon the levels, pray he'll live

Forever, write a sonnet of my own
To leave with him, afraid to be alone.

Today is Wednesday. Daisies on his bed --
White petals, with a periwinkle head --

Are withering in yellow cellophane.
There is no living thing, for all this rain.

There are a few short messages in lead --
None in my language -- praising what he said.

I leave my poem, believing if I tuck
It well beneath the flowerpots, with luck

My paper and the tissue stained with tears
And make-up might remain with him for years,

Then rise to rummage through my scented bag,
Until I reach the woven, linen rag.

They say that Wednesday's child is full of woe.
The woman leaves. I do not want to go.

At La Basilique du Sacré-Cœur de Montmartre

I looked out on Montmartre and I wept.
So many roofs of straight, slate gray and blue,
the terra-cotta stovepipes all that kept
a hint of warmth and roundness in the view.

I sank against the fencing and I wrote,
pulling down my hat's stiff, woven brim,
to pry the hemline of my overcoat
from where it had been caught on railing trim.

The simple motions of a simple soul
laboring to breathe at such a height --
ashamed, almost, unable to control
what caused the crowds no trouble at this sight.

We ordinary hordes, aboard this terrace:
musicians, jocks, performing artists, mimes,
so casually overlooking Paris
in covert, patient penance for our crimes.

My overwhelming flood of feeling gone,
I joined the pilgrimage, with drier peers,
lacking that protection from the sun
used nonchalantly to disguise my tears.

Requesting, "*S'il-vous plait, mais votre chapeau...*"
a greeting usher smiled, "...remove it, please,"
forbidding interruption in the flow
of visitants through clerics on their knees.

Thus we filed -- uncovered dust -- the dim
interior become my second veil.
The usher passed, I gripped my hat's bent brim.
We passed medallion images for sale.

The *Virgo Pacis* missing one wrought square
within the golden gateway to her shrine,
she nonetheless possessed the only prayer
petitioned from those seekers out of line.

We passed much holiness, but I returned,
revisiting the Virgin with her six
white, massive candles, upright and unburned
above the votives with their low, scarred wicks.

To a Woman on the Metro

You know, the Paris underground will stare,
so pull your hat brim low, and hide your eyes.
To meet their gazes is to be aware
of hunger in a major city size
which you -- alone and fragile -- are unable
to satisfy, though your allure is great;
as great as that encountered in a fable,
perhaps as great as Paris, glimpsed this late.
And while your modesty must be commended,
your eagerness to please them with a smile
you do not recognize as being splendid,
they, too, are great as Paris -- and as vile.
One stop away, with one suggestive shove,
they will bruise Beauty, in pursuit of Love.

Seine Dirge

Say that she has gone to Paris in her sleep.
Kiss her closed, once-brown eyes, as the blue appears.
She has not made you promise her you will not weep.
Say that she has gone to Paris in her sleep.

Slowly, through the city of a thousand years,
Watch her cross the Pont Neuf waters, strange and deep,
Singing in a fertile key through sterile tears,
Neither knowing, neither caring now who hears.

Tell the parish priests and prophets she will keep
Watch from heights at Notre Dame she no more fears,
Calling forward, counting, both, God's costly sheep.
Say that she has gone to Paris in her sleep.

Fleur de Lis

II.   Fugue and Funerary

For Charlie Hebdo

"Terrorists Strike Heart of Paris
Gunmen Flee After Killing 12 at Satirical Newspaper"
International New York Times

And now, these precious entities shall never perish,
But having gained the recognition and the ruth
Of all the world, will linger in eternal youth –
Their humor undeniable, their colors garish.

Their caricatures, underneath a simple, squarish
Title, block out blasphemies; squat and uncouth
And too rebellious, but blended well with truth:
Tastelessness raised to a fine art form to cherish.

And how can any wheat so pure sift through such chaff,
Eliciting a guilty pleasure and a laugh –
That cheerful act by which mankind may be made free?

Belied, their anarchy and anger towards the normal.
Recorded onto history, we plainly see
Those hands, those mannerisms – manicured and formal!

One Brother Suffers
(for my sons)

One brother suffers, and another brother—
and then a third—is standing by his side.
This is the surest sign to any mother
by which her sons can be identified.

Not eyes of blue that make a sibling's match;
nor cow-licked hair that sports the same brown curl;
not that they all watch films with Cumberbatch;
nor that they each pursue the same good girl.

One brother has been singled out to suffer.
Here is a certain sign the same womb bore them:
Two more arrive like angels—bigger, tougher.
And for this act of blood, all saints adore them.

Into the Cross

Into the cross at the altar I fixed
blossoms of apricot, ruffled carnation.
Thrust through its chicken wire cover, they mixed
humbly with those from the huge congregation.
Under your arm, Jesus, into that side
brutally slashed, underneath Your bowed head.
Dwarfed by the white daisies and the black-eyed
Susans and roses of blood or true red.
What will the ministers do with it since?
What does one do when the service is over,
ever with You -- brother, lover, and prince?
I can imagine them, pulling the clover,
flowers and fencing, to place it in storage --
pastors and volunteers, shaking with laughter.
Lord -- I am liquid, the color of porridge.
Mutely, I go to my pew in the rafter,
thinking, "My dream, my remembrance, my loss..."
everyone pausing, to let me move through,
everyone singing, "The Old Rugged Cross,"
back to my dry bench, besotted with You.

Non Omnis Moriar
"Not all of me shall die"
--Horace

This is my grief in secret: he is gone
Who lies against me twilight until dawn.
I breathe in pollen with his body's vapors.
I shelve his books and organize old papers,
Retrieve his Wall Street Journals from the lawn,

Brew coffee and pretend to hear him yawn,
Reprove some fashion magazine, or fawn
Over "Faust." I dredge his cress with Spanish capers.
This is my grief in secret.
No longer are the curtains ever drawn;

No longer are the wall lamps ever on.
I rub his limp hands, light the bees' wax tapers,
Remembering he called them "stamen rapers."
"My heart in halves," I tell him, "has been sawn."
This is my grief in secret.

***

His warmth and vigor lost, I took him cold.
His heart at rest, the hurried last bell tolled,
I hushed his *rigor mortis*, and the hearse
Averted, took him as I vowed: for worse –
Past even sickness and disease, to hold.

In flesh, the sedulous maggot goes enrolled –
But when the flies arrived, how could I fold
The sheet across his face, which grew more terse,
His warmth and vigor lost?
Jaundiced to a learned, mosaic gold.

My solace being unseen and controlled,
Those acts of satisfaction that immerse
My pain in pleasure – how could he curse
What was consensual? To be consoled,
His warmth and vigor lost.

***

His half being known now as The Other Side,
I roll and question him: hard-boiled or fried
The eggs? Then slide my fingers round a bone,
Evening my voice to monotone.
Subside, the motion cautions me, *subside.*

The white rose eulogizing him, beside
The lilies in the upper hall, has dried –
Funereal perfumes much like my own.
His half being known,
I clip the blooms and bring them like a bride

To emptiness which I must climb astride.
There are the rose, my cloying French cologne,
I wave the first, pretend to hear him groan,
His half being known.
One slip and suddenly, it is inside.

***

In intimacy not fulfilled before,
One wonders what corruption holds in store,
Now I am free, and he is unaware
Of how the strands of his still-growing hair
Are traced, and how explored his every pore;

How, entering the room, I slam the door
To strain against bereavement more and more,
Gripping the posts and rocking like a chair
In intimacy,
My boring, furthest love brought to the fore;

How he knows neither sovereignty nor
What it is like to feel the tendons tear,
Nor has capacity now to compare,
But seeps – like me, until the lungs are sore
In intimacy.

***

I will still kiss that other half until
My passions, like his own, becoming still,
I have surrendered dumbly to the dead –
A crossed romantic on a creaking bed,
Ecstatic with a stiffened mouth to fill.

Ambitious, arch, each afternoon, I will
Be teased by weeds beyond the windowsill,
Flourishing beyond that withered head
I will still kiss;
At dusk, I will select a sedge to kill,

Symbolic of the puritan. What shrill,
Long, crying winds might be destroyed, instead,
When night descends, the trickle of blood red
From chill lips mocking mine – a dreaded thrill
I will still kiss.

The Spirit of Kees at Preservation Hall

He looks down in my eyes, down, steps from Bourbon,
To extricate – as no one ever has –
Asylum for a night, despite the urban
Assault late evening ushers in with jazz.
He finds no noise within them, just a hint
Of temper which has perished but returned;
No *schadenfreude* shining here like flint;
No nest of wasps to be disturbed and burned.
Aghast, he vanishes, unwanted daughter
Discerned. He fades like film, both elbows bent,
His left hand round a gin and tonic water,
His right arm round my mother, Malcontent –
Self-abnegation vanquishing by fear
That strength through which we struggle to appear.

Lift My Head

Lift my chin, Lord,
Say to me,
"You are not who
You feared to be,
Not Hecate, quite,
With howling sound,
Torch held upright,
Black acolyte
Gone underground.

Not consort to
Persephone,
Not Queen of Night
Who, hurling through
The highest blue
Of blessed airs
Your gruesome prayers,
Hit Heaven's Queen –
A crone, crone of the unforeseen.
Not chthonic-skinned
And triple-tongued,
And lunar-lung'd."

Lift my chin, Lord,
Let me mend –
A mother to the damned,
A friend
Pledged to the dead,
Daughter adored
By those abhorred,
Grown through the grave. Lord,
Lift my head.

Triolet

Believing in the Eucharist,
My faith affirmed within the Host,
I welcome -- with an upturned wrist,
Believing in the Eucharist --
These elements, to take amidst
The Father, Son and Holy Ghost,
Believing in the Eucharist,
My faith affirmed within the Host.

Grieving Angel
for Wil Mills

Outstretched is useless; and for all this length
The sculptor has embedded in her form
Of stone, she is a statue without strength--
Cold in a southern crypt of humid, warm,
Diffused light, seen through stained blue atmosphere,
As though she had been washed up in a storm,
Some figure purged from Twelfth Night or King Lear,
Whose heated, inner sorrowing none hear.

To symbolize the helplessness of loss,
Is she not perfect in a social sense?
Familiar to us both, amid the moss
And mosquitoes, blanched to the most intense
White, one could surmise her hidden face
To be so inexpressive of offense
As to invite disaster, with no trace
Of blame or accusation--fat with grace.

Whatever pain we might protract is mental.
She is the product of a poet's skills,
Like you and me--too poisonously gentle
For transplant in a world of living wills.
As far as we can tell, she has no heart,
And we, no heart to speculate what mills
Beneath her surface, superficial art.
We take the top alone, and come apart.

Would it be terrifying?

Would it be terrifying, to be mine?
There would be such reciprocation, such
reprisal night, day; I would let you clutch
My life each dying moment, to define
The limits of my tongue, and set white wine
Or red, or rose, in front of me as much
As you decided necessary, touch
My ghostly glass. I would imbibe and dine,
Imprint transparent fingers, call your name
All night, each night, to any who could hear,
Until – expression perishing – your fame
Were echoes of sweet nothings in each ear;
That place to which we came, one and the same –
Illusions, each conspicuously clear.

The Ballad of St. James Infirmary

The path was thick with thistle, mum.
  Beneath a cypress tree,
A sign defined where I had come:
  St. James Infirmary.

A fortnight's passing since All Souls',
  Rainwater rushed through gutters,
Down pointed, crescent, Creole poles,
  And green Parisian shutters;

Sluiced through my hood, to my loose hair,
  Inducing me to think,
Water, water, everywhere,
  Nor any drop to drink.

A serum I had sipped alone
  From August through October
Zipped at a bone, mild moonlight shone,
  Recalcitrant and sober.

So aster-strangled was its rot,
  So vivid its chipped brick,
So chalk its walkways, I forgot
  It once had housed the sick.

Two questions posed themselves, as clear
  As though they were a text:
When would appear the thing I fear,
  And what would happen next?

Vining Louisiana vetch –
  Entwining black through white –
Became an animated sketch.
  The entrance came in sight.

It, too, viewed through each louvered blade
  In dripping shades of gray,
Reclined behind a colonnade,
  Bleached, in deep decay.

Beside the oak-encircled porch
  Were idling sixteen mares;
Above, a torch. One soot-traced scorch
  Encroached on outer stairs.

Against my temple, I had set
  A Russian REX revolver,
Speckled and wet, to play roulette –
  The rain, no pain dissolver.

Throughout my coming, I had spun
  Its chamber in my mind:
Six to one, the odds my gun
  Would falter, as designed.

Surprised to find on Magazine—
  A street well-known, I swore –
This hospice where an inn had been
  A century before,

I sashayed past a ghost plant urn,
  Freak, bleak accommodations
And spider fern, in lagged return,
  Unused to please impatience;

Arriving, through that sterile air
  Crucial to institutions,
Inside a charnel chamber, bare
  But for some spilled solutions.

In front of me, a form – supine
  Upon a long, white table –
Lay flat and fine in cold outline,
  One toe tagged with a label.

Now, close your eyes, I thought. Those eyes
  Were my eyes, and those lips
Would neither frighten me, nor rise,
  The hue of dried rose hips.

How unmistakable, the tilt
  Of that indifferent head!
How sharp those shoulder blades, the wilt
  Of pose! How still. How dead.

A satire underneath a sheet:
  Unchanging, stiff, and strange,
Fair, frigid, sweet, and too discreet,
  With last rites to arrange.

So noting, let me be the first
  To give my last directions:
In parting, let there be no thirst.
  Perform no vivisections.

Six kinds of wine have at my wake,
  Six felines to meow.
Play early, "The Unfortunate Rake."
  I have no interest how.

And do not bury me in blue.
　　Choose black, or any other.
Blue was the venerable hue
　　　In which I laid my mother.

I always did admire those pleats
　　Of satin, puffed and tight,
Which imitated wedding sheets
　　In subtle shades of white.

Lay me in such. Display a wreath
　　Of sweet alyssum near
My head, stone urns of thyme beneath,
　　To make the scents austere.

My guest book signed, do not assume
　　All this has been enough.
I wonder if there *could* be room
　　To floor the floral stuff.

Invite an epileptic horde,
　　The lepers, pagans, lames,
Reciting – as to lure Our Lord –
　　My ballad of St. James.

Miniature: The Virgin Model

Beneath the robe, her heels and toes are bare,
An introspective effigy in whose
Imaginary sandal-flat-soled shoes
No martyr nor prospective saint would dare
To walk in, work in, lose what she would lose.
And of her mold, one might as well despair.
Below a cloak of apricot, her hair
Is parted as the Red Sea, no eyelash
To soften or obscure her doe-eyed gaze.
There is no marble in her to amaze.
The residents could call her stable trash.

O Mistress to a god you could not hold,
Touch, hear with your own ears and understand;
Inquisitive, but in the end resolved
To scandal, shame – I see you cross the sand
With bleeding, limping feet, as though on salt.
And I invoke you, formal to a fault –
That fault we share, of which we are absolved.

At Asphodel Plantation

Do not disturb me; do not hold your breath
for my reply. I am no more alive,
and shall be un-persuaded, after death.
I have been out to lunch from nine to five,
in a Cajun kitchen, on a wobbly table.
How could a crushed narcissus bloom survive --
like all the finest, lovely but unstable --
beneath a showcase poster of Clark Gable,
aloft on cayenne stems, and garlic chive?
Don't dig for me, and do not call me "hot"
because in this humidity, I thrive.
The slightest steam escapes the lobster pot,
and I am wilted in a dish too rich
for daffodils, picked from a drainage ditch.

To the Estranged

Sometimes a person may be tempted to accept
neglect from those who seem to qualify as great,
assuming ignorance and cold to be his fate;
resigned to anonymity, dejected, swept
away by bitter bankruptcy, and those adept
at arrogance; to be inclined to overrate
those privileged successors of the fourth estate,
believing roses sprout where the Elite have stepped.
Bohemian! The toe of the Establishment
is pink adobe rooted in a pool of spittle,
eroding slowly by an unobstructed drip
from spread lips, having hardened, curled without relent.
This hulk, to hold its structure, must stand non-committal,
and may not move to save itself – head, hand, nor hip.

Fleur de Lis

III.   From *Les Fleurs du Mal*
poems of Charles Baudelaire

Burial
by Charles Baudelaire

If on a night of sinking gloom
A Christian, out of charity,
Inters your praised corpse in a tomb
Behind some old debris,

The hour when the distant suns,
Becoming dense, have closed their eyes,
The spider there, its web has spun,
The viper made its little one;

On your convicted head, the cries
of wolverines you then will hear
lamenting the entire year,

And some famished witches then,
The plotting of black, swindling men,
And old lechers as they leer.

Conversation
by Charles Baudelaire

You are a lovely sky of autumn, clear and rose!
But inside me, grief is rising, like the sea,
Leaving as it ebbs upon my lip morose,
Bitter culinary silts of memory.

--Vainly does your hand slide on my swooning breast;
This place it is seeking has been pillaged, friend,
By the woman's tooth-and-claw ferociousness.
My heart was eaten by the beasts. Let searching end.

My heart is like a palace ransacked by a riot;
One gets drunk there, one pulls hair there, one is quiet!
--Around your naked neck is swimming a perfume!...

O Beauty, scourge of hearts, this thing you would consume!
With your eyes of fire, akin to brilliant feasts,
Burn to ash these remnants salvaged by the beasts!

The Poison
by Charles Baudelaire

Wine knows how to cover the most sordid place
With the miraculous,
And makes a portico emerge more fabulous
In the red-gold of its haze,
Like skies at sundown, set in nebulas.

Opium expands to that which has no bound,
Stretches endlessly,
Time deepens, excavating sensuality,
Pleasures black and un-profound
Overflow the soul beyond capacity.

None of this can match the bane which swells
In your eyes, your eyes of green,
Lakes in which my trembling, backwards soul is seen...
To embittered wells,
Like crowds in need of water, come my dreams.

None of this is equal to the vile, immense
Slavering bite of yours,
Which stupefies my soul without remorse,
And carting dizziness,
Rolls it in a faint toward death's shores!

The Revenant
by Charles Baudelaire

Like angels with ferocious sight,
I will return with shades of night
To the recess where you reside
And noiselessly towards you glide;

Dark one, I will give to you
Kisses frigid as the moon,
Like a serpent crawling through
A snake pit, my caress of you.

When arrives the pallid dawn,
You will find my presence gone,
Where the weather chills till night.

As others would by tenderness
Over your youth and consciousness,
Me, I want to rule by fright.

A Martyr
by Charles Baudelaire

In the midst of bottles, flasks, among some marbles,
Some material of gold,
Furniture well-rounded, scented gowns on tables
Trailing into lavish fold,

Where, as within a greenhouse, air in the room
Is dangerous and unto death,
Where the dying sprays of flowers in glass tombs
Exhale their final breath,

A corpse without a head releases, like a flood
Upon the thirst-quenched pillow
And avaricious toile, a red and living blood,
Drunk in as by a meadow.

Similar to pallid visions which birth shade
And which enchain our eyes,
The head, with its amassing of the somber braid,
And its jewels beyond price,

Like a buttercup upon the bedside stand
Rests; and, like the twilight,
A vague look, white and at a loss to understand,
Escapes its upturned sight.

And upon the bed, abandoned perfectly,
Unscrupulous, the nude trunk, loose,
Whose secret splendor and whose beauty fatally
Gifted him with nature's use.

One rose stocking, as if a reminder, stays,
Edged in gold against a thigh;
The garter set so as to dart a secret gaze
From a flaming, diamond eye.

The singular appearance of this solitude
And languoressness therof
Reveal in a grand portrait, like her attitude
With tempting eyes, a dark love,

Unfamiliar banquets and illicit blisses
Which please the demonic shapes
Swarming by the fullness of infernal kisses,
Swimming in the folds of drapes.

However from the stricken edge, to see how fragile
To the shoulder, thin and elegant,
The hip pointed a little, the waistline agile
As an agitated serpent,

She is young as yet! Her character in umbrage,
Her senses by boredom snared,
Were soul and sense half-opened to the warped baggage
Of desire which has strayed and erred?

That vindictive man you could not satiate
 Despite such love, while living,
With his immense desire, did he saturate
Your flesh, made lifeless and obliging?

Respond, impure cadaver! By a stiff braid tress,
From a feverish arm, arise,
Tell me, on your cold teeth, gross head, did he press
The ultimate goodbyes?

--Far from curious judges, far from impure nation,
Far from the world which will find fault,
Sleep in peacefulness, sleep calmly, strange creation,
In your mysterious vault;

Your husband runs throughout the world, your form, immortal,
Wakeful near him in his bed;
Doubtless as concerning you, he will be loyal,
Constant until he is dead.

Women Damned
by Charles Baudelaire

Within the lamps' pale, languid limpidness,
Upon deep cushions, impregnated full of scents,
Hippolyte dreamed of the potent caress
Which raised the drapery upon her innocence.
She searched, with a tempest-troubled eye,
For her naivete, from heaven far withdrawn,
As though a voyager regarding sky,
Having turned the head around towards an azure dawn.

Her stupor, somnolent and teary-eyed,
The air of brokenness, the dismal sensuousness,
Like weapons spent, the conquered arms thrown wide,
All serviced, all befit her fragile loveliness.

Extended at her feet, serene and gay,
With her desirous eyes, Delphine was smoldering,
Like a strong animal surveys its prey
Once having made the mark of its initial sting.

Strong beauty on its knees in front of frail,
Superb, she stretched herself around her wantonly
In such a way as seeming to inhale
Sweet thankfulness, receive the wine of victory.

The canticle which sings of pleasure, mute,
She searched for, in her pallid victim's eye,
And that sublime, infinite gratitude
Which exits from the eyelid like a lengthy sigh.

"Hippolyte, what do you have to say,
Dear heart, about these things? Do you now comprehend
This holy gift you must not give away,
Your finest rose, blown, withered by a violent wind?

Lightly as mayflies do my kisses hover,
Caressing grand, transparent waters after dusk,
And like a truck would be those of your lover,
As though he harrowed with a ploughshare, digging ruts.
Like a heavy horse's harness, without grace,
Or like the cruel yoke of cattle they will pass,
Hippolyte, my sister! Turn your face,
You, my soul and heart, my all, my other half,

Turn to me your star-filled eyes of azure!
For one enchanting glance, a holy healing cream,
Will I lift up a veil of darker pleasure,
And I will then sedate you in an endless dream!"

But then, the young head raised, Hippolyte:
"I don't regret, and do not feel ingratitude,
I suffer, my Delphine, anxiety,
As after tasting terrible, nocturnal food.

I feel dissolving on me dreadful doors,
And apparitions scattered in a black battalion,
Who wish to drive me on a risky course,
Closed off from any exit on the blood horizon.

Are we committing actions which are strange?
Explain my terror, if you can, and my distress.
I shiver with fright when you say, 'My angel!'
And feel my mouth to go towards you nonetheless.

Don't look at me in such a way, my thought!
You whom I always love, my sister by election,
When you would be the trap by which I'm caught,
As well as the commencement of my perdition!"

Delphine shook out her miserable mane,
And stamping with her feet, as on a stand of iron,
Look fatal, gave her answer in a despot's strain:
"Who so, in love's vicinity, dares speak of hell-fire?
Forever be the idle dreamer doomed,
Preferring the premier, in her stupidity,
Obsessed with unsolved problems, and consumed
With mingling the affairs of love with decency!

The one who, like a mystic, would unite
The darkness with the day, the shaded with the warm,
Will never from the red sun, Love, have light
By which to heat her paralytic form!

Go, then, to find a stupid fiance!
Run off, to give your pure heart to his cruel caress,
And, filled with horror and remorse, and gray,
Stigmatized, you will bring again to me your breasts...

One may please but one master here below!"
But pouring out immense distress, the mademoiselle
Cried suddenly, "I feel swelled in my soul
A pit without a bottom: my heart is this hell!

As deep as space, like a volcano, fiery!
Nothing will sate the moaning of this monster's need,
And nothing cools the thirsting of the Dirae
Who, lanterns in their hands, are burning till they bleed.

That our closed drapes divide us from creation
And that the lassitude accompanies the rest!
In your deep throat, I long for my destruction,
To find the freshness of the grave upon your breast!"

--Descend, lamentable victims, go down
Upon the pathway to eternal hell, descend,
Plunge into the depression most profound,
Where all crimes are beaten by sky-forsaken wind,

Mad shadows, run till your desire is spent.
Boil pell-mell with noises of a thunderstorm;
This rabidness you never can content,
And from your pleasures will your punishment be born.

Never will a new ray brighten your caverns,
By fissures in the walls of feverish miasmas
Filtering in, so as to light the lanterns
And penetrate your bodies' horrible aromas.

Your amusement's sour sterility
Perverts your thirst, and stiffens you into a hag,
And your lustfulness, with a wind-like fury,
Causes your flesh to slap you like an aging flag.

Far from humanity, condemned, astray,
Traverse through deserts, like the foxes wander through;
Making your fortune, souls in disarray,
And fleeing the infinity inside of you!

Mist and Rain
by Charles Baudelaire

O ends of autumn, winters, springs of mud-soaked days,
Seasons of enticement! You I love and praise,
Enveloping my spirit and perception thus
Within a vague tomb, shrouded in the vaporous.
Where bleak winds from the south play on this august plain,
Through lengthy nights against the grating weathervane,
My spirit, better than the time when summer brings
Renewing warmth, will open wide its raven wings.
The funereal spirit finds no other thing more sweet
Where frost has been descending for the longest time,
O weak, anemic seasons, regents of our clime,
That pale appearance of your shadows made complete,
--If not this, on a moonless evening, head to head,
Rocking to sleep the sadness on an unsafe bed.

A Carcass
by Charles Baudelaire

Recall the thing we saw beside the bypass
Diverging from the trail ahead
This fair, sweet summer day, my soul, a carcass
Repulsive on a pebbled bed.

Like a lustful woman lacking passion,
The poisons hot with perspiration,
The legs in air and spread in cynic fashion,
Its belly full of exhalation.

The sunlight shone on this disintegration
As if to cook it to a point,
And to return one-hundredfold to Nature
All of this she had conjoined.

The sky observed this splendid carrion
As though it were a blooming flower.
One would expect to faint upon the lawn
The stench of it had been so sour.

Around its putrid abdomen, flies flitted
Where black battalion larvae scattered,
Dispersing like a firm and heavy liquid
The length of it alive and tattered.

All this, with breaking sounds was pouring forth
Like waves arising and abating.
Swelled by vague breath, one should have said the corpse
Remained alive by procreating.

This world was rendering a strange refrain
Like rushing water and the winds,
Or rhythms of a winnower whose grain
Within his basket beats and spins.

No more than dream, the figures were effaced,
An illustration coming slow
On forgetful cloth the artist must have traced
Achieved through memory alone.

Rearward of the rock, a nervous mongrel
With a maddened eye looked on,
Awaiting the moment to retrieve the morsel
Abandoned from the skeleton.

And yet, this filth is like what you will feature,
This horrible infection,
Star of my eyes, sunlight of my nature,
You, my angel and my passion!

Yes! Such as this you'll be, o graceful queen!
Following the final rite,
When you have gone below the flowery green,
Between the molded bones to blight.

Then, o my beauty! notify the insects
Eating, kissing you, that above,
I have preserved the form and perfect essence
Of my corrupted love!

The Ideal
by Charles Baudelaire

It never will be beauties out of these vignettes,
Damaged products, swindles of a century,
These feet in boots, the fingertips to castanets,
Which could be satisfying to a soul like me.
I leave to Paul Gavarni, poet of chlorosis,
His troop of beauties from the hospital to squeal,
For I cannot find within these pallid roses
A flower with resemblance to my red ideal.
To the heart profound as an abyss within this clime,
It's you, Lady MacBeth, soul powerful at crime,
Aeschylus's dream in winds born from the south;
Or you, grand Night, child of Michelangelo's,
That torso peaceful in a strange repose,
Whose charms are fashioned at the Titan's mouth!

The Skeleton Worker
by Charles Baudelaire

In the anatomic plates
Which trail along this dusty dock,
Where many a cadaverous book
Sleeps like a mummy, aged of dates,

Engravings through which gravity
And through old artists' skillfulness,
Despite the subject's gloominess,
Communicated Beauty,

One sees, to make more integral
These horrifying mysteries,
Digging as if ploughmen, these
Flayed of skin, and skeletal.

II.

From this ground you dig into,
Churls, funereal and resigned,
From the efforts of your spine
Or else from your stripped sinew,

Say, what strange crop do you reap,
Convicts taken from the grave,
And for which farmer do you have
To draw, whose granary to heap?

Do you desire (hard to endure
A fate, an omen definite!)
To show that even in the pit
The promised slumber is not sure,

That by the Nothing, we're betrayed,
That everything, Death, too, will lie
And that for all eternity
Alas! Perhaps we will be made

Upon some continent unreal
To skin the adamantine dust,
And with a heavy spade to thrust
Beneath our bare and bloody heel?

The Death of Lovers
by Charles Baudelaire

We'll have beds full of faint scents for ourselves,
Divans unfathomable as the tombs,
And, broken open for us on the shelves
Beneath the finest sky, exotic blooms.

Their heat intensified increasingly,
Reflecting both our spirits within,
Two massive torches our two hearts will be,
Their double brightness each a mirrored twin.

One evening made of rose and mystic blue,
As though we sobbed a lengthy, charged *adieu,*
We will exchange one single flash of light;

Half-opening the portals later on,
An angel will revive, with true delight,
The tarnished glass and flames which once were gone.

Fleur de Lis

IV.   Paris to Orleans

Transformation

If Paris were plunged into pitch,
a Roman shade rendering solemn
the whole of the Seine, quai and ditch,
Palais Royal's each oddly-cut column;
if – shut in a chic Chanel stitch –
the city were fashioned with screens,
in its handiwork, nary a niche,
then Paris might be New Orleans.

If moss grew from plane trees like hair
grey and aggressive with grime –
locks of some grim sorcière
granted to see the sublime –
humidity swamping the air
brashly with pestilent sheens:
black glasses on, one could swear
Paris had been New Orleans.

After dusk on the Champs Elysées,
in a bi-level building, beef frying,
at a bistro beside a café,
the cashier slams his drawer, denying
one's request for espresso, to say
that there are no more, as though lying –
gawky, tall, not yet out of his teens.
So one thanks him, and smiles, "*Bonne soirée*,"
finds *au lait*, like in far New Orleans.

At the break of day, vendors with crates
carry fruits and legumes into shops,
seeming bravely resigned to their fates,
where distraction needs lather and mops.
Dainty scribbles describe the day's plates
on boards tasseled and backed with moreens,
and the language of love re-instates
one's belief this could be New Orleans.

In the Madeleine district, the wrought
iron rails masquerading as lace,
citrine barriers – plastic and taut –
tape construction work. Slowing one's pace
for the pregnant and aged, as one ought,
the displaced and the poor-without-means
beg one blind for the bags one has bought
in this Paris become New Orleans.

And I scuttle past hatters and glovers
unaccounted for, brushing the gentle
and the harsh in this city for lovers,
with the miniscule and monumental;
unidentified, under the cover
of a heaven that cries as it cleans –
at once native and transcontinental
between Paris and my New Orleans.

Chant Royal

Every day, throughout the day,
By artificial fire, I see
Directions which I cannot say
Are this or that, with certainty.
On teas of ginger and Dong Quai,
Far from the French blue of the sky,
Soft haloes from the hallway throw
Their glazes in a coral glow
Which might as well be brown or blue
As far as I'm concerned, I know.
My mind is pigmented with you.

It is an inner room. No ray
Of sunlight by the least degree
Creeps across its dull parquet
Replete with tins and Rose Chablis.
This deep obscurity whereby
Fineness is foreign to the eye
Ceased to depress me long ago.
I rue the sight it ruined – oh!
These bogus "auras" brought to view.
And yet, I turn the burners low.
My mind is pigmented with you.

A blackened *roux*, a shrimp soufflé,
Cold syrup from the honeybee,
Cane sugar from some Cajun bay –
These comprise my recipe;
A sprig of tarragon gone dry.
With usage, they de-mystify
The murkiness through which I go
About my frying, sly and slow.
I stir the stockpot, froth and stew,
The fast beignets from packaged dough.
My mind is pigmented with you.

When time has come to toss away
The rotted peels in company
With grease and various decay,
Where do you figure you will be?
Inside this scullery where I
Must blend with butter till I die,
My fingers slick with oleo,
One molecule from plastic? No.
But, going blind by steps, the hue
Of all things hesitant to show,
My mind is pigmented with you.

How much sagacity has gray
De-saturation meant to me!
What perfect vision could convey!
What wonder and sincerity!
But while they might be faulty, my
Impressions are not each a lie.
Despite all efforts to re-sew,
Sight is a garment we outgrow,
And color is not always true –
A minor complication, though.
My mind is pigmented with you.

Bourbon Street Love Sonnet

Averse to leave you, never to forget
The one alone in whom I am complete,
I have withdrawn to lawless Bourbon Street,
Called on the Creole sun, and watched it set.

Though having left you, I shall not have let
You go, but, making light, and being sweet,
I listen to the crowds as they repeat
Clichés, and to the snare, and clarinet.

Amid these French faces, this wrought lace iron --
One hundred hardened hustlers in attendance,
Perhaps a figment of my memory --
I've stopped in shops opposite the siren,
To count the cost and change of independence:
A horned horse in a made menagerie.

City in Bleak

(New Orleans, Autumn)

Poor palm in the steam of a water treatment tower,
and a woman waves a white cloth twelve floors up;
plump rock doves on the corner of Decatur
and Conti gobble crumbs hurled from a cup.

The Faulkner Bookstore dealer--sweater-vested
and spectacled--is happy Chekov sells,
inscribes our thin receipt by hand, reclines
against the tatting of his chair and tells
us to avoid the tank outside, to east,
sweeping through Pirate's Alley. I hear gulls,
trains, crows--the Tao of common life at least.

I search the galleries and Quarter racks
for subtle postcards, postcards I could send
to anyone without embarrassment,
whose artistry defies both rite and trend.

I find Monsieur Clauzade, arrived from France,
whose bijou girls and beach scenes seem to tear
the walls with their primary colors, and Sebille
with shocking poppies, scarlet as a flare,
on scads of yellow paint.

                    The convent halls
alone are left to find, though I foresee
postcards will be collected slowly, streetcars
be tardy, and time not enough for me.

From the French Quarter

A few things I have found grow ever sweeter,
Remaining fresh and free, and never tiring:
The Yankee yelling, "Stella!" down St. Peter;
The cayenne and Tabasco peppers firing
My palate with humidity and heat;
The washboard bands with fiddlers playing Dixie;
The chimes from balconies on Chartres Street;
The living, silver figures – linen pixie
With painted, stiff tuxedos on the Square;
The artist with his easel on Rue Royal;
These sounds one won't encounter anywhere
But here – exotic, soulful, loud and loyal,
Which strike me, by their age, as ever new,
Like Giza, and the pyramids, and you.

New Orleans

This town has little time for snow;
Once perhaps, per century,
Which bakes away next day: brief dough.
This town has little time for snow.
Its gentlemen and ladies go
Like fire ants of the *fleur-de-lis*.
This town has little time for snow;
Once perhaps, per century.

Madam, for what reason, this atrocity?

Madam, for what reason, this atrocity?
These captives, what they need, enchained in lead,
are names, names recorded in tranquility,

more of your benevolent restraint, instead
of your exasperation, of your spite,
who serve to you your evening wine and bread.

From above, I hear cries of those without delight,
of souls without hope, imagination –
a clean spirit, quickly dying. Dead from fright?

One who in life was black, now faded phantom white.

A Louisiana Coronation

Today the French laureate
takes his place
among the swamp people.

And the ice
the ice of winter
remains upon our rooftops
and upon our fingers
here, here still
even above the tropics.

A child sleeps
even in America,
dreaming of the lily,
that flower lily
through which he will be transported
transported forever

from the humidity
from mud and shrimp
from hurricanes and the course
of destruction of poverty
to a foreign country
to a feast of kings
and poets.

About the author:

Jennifer Reeser is author of <u>An Alabaster Flask</u>, winner of the Word Press First Book Prize, <u>Winterproof</u>, <u>Sonnets from the Dark Lady and Other Poems</u>, a finalist for the Donald Justice Prize, and bestselling epic, <u>The Lalaurie Horror</u>. Her poems, critical essays, and translations of Cherokee, French and Russian literature have appeared in journals including *Poetry, The Hudson Review, The Formalist, Light Quarterly, Able Muse, The National Review* and *The Dark Horse*, and have been gathered in anthologies such as <u>Measure for Measure,</u> in Penguin/Random House Publisher's *Everyman's Library* series, in Longman's textbook, <u>An Introduction to Poetry</u> (edited by X.J. Kennedy and Dana Gioia), and <u>Poets Translate Poets: A Hudson Review Anthology</u>. They also have been translated into Urdu, Hindi, Persian and the Czech language. Her work has received critical praise from Nobel Prize nominee Nasir Ahmed Naseer. X.J. Kennedy wrote that her first collection "ought to have been a candidate for a Pulitzer." She has served as a seminar moderator, mentor and manuscript consultant on faculty with the West Chester Poetry Conference, and lives amid the bayous of southern Louisiana with the fiction writer, Jason Reeser and her black cat Baca.

For more information about Jennifer's poetry please visit her website at <u>jenniferreeser.com</u>

Now Available from Saint James Infirmary Books. Look for these books on Jennifer's website or check with your local bookseller. Also available for Kindle at Amazon.com.

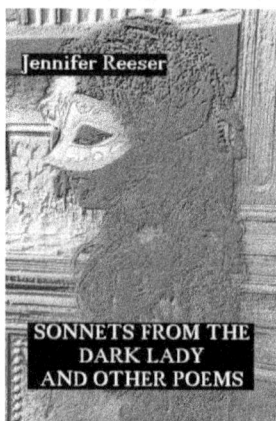

"...a stunning collection of top-notch poetry..."

— Joseph S. Salemi,
Editor, *TRINACRIA*

"I love these sculpted and energetic poems, full of drama and wit."

—Michael Potemra,
Literary Editor,
National Review

A macabre, paranormal tour of New Orleans, exquisitely beautiful in its craft and disturbingly potent in its judgment. Read at your peril.

A top-selling Epic Poem at Amazon.com.

Cited as a resource by world-renowned, French criminologist, Stéphane Burgoin, a foremost authority on serial killers.

Non-Fiction from Jason and Jennifer Reeser:

Saint James Infirmary Presents the travel memoir

Room With Paris View

"The detail, the curious footfalls of the Reesers are a joy to follow, even when they are regularly lost. There are many confused steps, but none are wasted. You see, this really is a guide book for those who want good ideas, but certainly don't want guiding."—author Richard Bunning

Jason and Jennifer Reeser arrived in Paris on a windy day in April. For the next two weeks, as rain fell every day, they explored the city of Eiffel, Rodin, Picasso, the Louvre, Notre Dame Cathedral, Sacré Cœur, Saint-Sulpice, and Père Lachaise Cemetery. Choosing to steer clear of hotels and canned tours, they rented an apartment on the top floor of a six-floor walk-up. Despite the cold and the rain, despite their lack of traveling experience, they were determined to see all they could of the city that inspired the likes of Vincent Van Gogh, Claude Monet, Charles Baudelaire, Victor Hugo, Oscar Wilde, Emile Zola, and Ernest Hemingway.

For anyone who has ever thought that a trip to Paris would be full of rude waiters, bad food, and insufferable crowds, this will set the record straight.

Full of advice for first-time travelers, literary and historical notes, as well as an entertaining account of their views on art, culture, cuisine, and the people of Paris (both the locals and the tourists), *Room With Paris View* will certainly give the reader a new perspective on the City of Light.